D0346641

# MASS FOR HARD TIMES

TONBRIDGE SCHOOL LIBRARY

R15053M0502

# Also available

POETRY BY R.S. THOMAS

*Selected Poems 1946-1968* (Hart-Davis, MacGibbon, 1973;
   paperback edition, Bloodaxe Books, 1986)
*What is a Welshman?* (Christopher Davies, 1974)
*Between Here and Now* (Macmillan, 1981)
*Later Poems* (Macmillan, 1984)
*Ingrowing Thoughts* (Seren Books, 1985)
*Counterpoint* (Bloodaxe Books, 1990)
*Collected Poems* (Dent, 1993)

PROSE BY R.S. THOMAS

*Selected Prose.* ed. Sandra Anstey (Seren Books, 1983;
   expanded edition, 1992)
*Neb*, ed. Gwenno Hywyn (Gwasg Gwynedd, 1985)

ESSAYS ON R.S. THOMAS

*Critical Writings on R.S. Thomas*, ed. Sandra Anstey
   (Seren Books, 1983)
D.Z. Phillips: *R.S. Thomas: Poet of the Hidden God*
   (Macmillan, 1986)
J.P. Ward: *The Poetry of R.S. Thomas* (Seren Books, 1987)
*R.S. Thomas Y Cawr Awenydd*, ed. M. Wynn Thomas
   (Gwasg Gomer, 1990)

# MASS FOR HARD TIMES

## R.S. THOMAS

BLOODAXE BOOKS

Copyright © R.S. Thomas 1992

ISBN: 1 85224 228 0  hardback edition
        1 85224 229 9  paperback edition

First published 1992 by
Bloodaxe Books Ltd,
P.O. Box 1SN,
Newcastle upon Tyne NE99 1SN.

Second impression 1994.

Bloodaxe Books Ltd acknowledges
the financial assistance of Northern Arts.

LEGAL NOTICE
All rights reserved. No part of this book may be
reproduced, stored in a retrieval system, or
transmitted in any form, or by any means, electronic,
mechanical, photocopying, recording or otherwise,
without prior written permission from Bloodaxe Books Ltd.
Requests to publish work from this book
must be sent to Bloodaxe Books Ltd.

R15053

821.91

25.581

Cover reproduction by V & H Reprographics, Newcastle upon Tyne.

Cover printing by J. Thomson Colour Printers Ltd, Glasgow.

Printed in Great Britain by
Bell & Bain Limited, Glasgow, Scotland.

*To the Memory of My Wife*
M.E. ELDRIDGE
1909–1991

# Contents

# Mass for Hard Times

## *Kyrie*

Because we cannot be clever and honest
and are inventors of things more intricate
than the snowflake – Lord have mercy.

Because we are full of pride
in our humility, and because we believe
in our disbelief – Lord have mercy.

Because we will protect ourselves
from ourselves to the point
of destroying ourselves – Lord have mercy.

And because on the slope to perfection,
when we should be half-way up,
we are half-way down – Lord have mercy.

## *Gloria*

From the body at its meal's end
and its messmate whose meal is beginning,
                              Gloria.

From the early and late cloud, beautiful and deadly
as the mushroom we are forbidden to eat,
                              Gloria.

From the stars that are but as dew
and the viruses outnumbering the star clusters,
                              Gloria.

From those waiting at the foot of the helix
for the rope-trick performer to come down,
                              Gloria.

Because you are not there
When I turn, but are in the turning,
                                    Gloria.

Because it is not I who look
but I who am being looked through,
                                    Gloria.

Because the captive has found the liberty
that eluded him while he was free,
                                    Gloria.

Because from the belief that nothing is nothing
it follows that there must be something,
                                    Gloria.

Because when we count we do not count
the moment between youth and age,
                                    Gloria.

And because, when we are overcome,
we are overcome by nothing,
                                    Gloria.


*Credo*

I believe in God
the Father (Is he married?)
I believe in you, the almighty,
who can do anything
you wish. (Forget that irony
of the imponderable.) Rid, therefore
(if there are not too many
of them), my intestine
of the viruses that against
(in accordance with? Ah, horror!)
your will are in occupation
of its defences. I call
on you, as I have done
often before (why repeat,
if he is listening?) to show
you are master of secondary

causation. (What has physics to do
with the heart's need?) Am I
too late, then, with my language?
Are symbols to be in future
the credentials of our approach?
(And how contemporary
is the Cross, that long-bow drawn
against love?) My questions
accumulate in the knowledge
it is words are the kiss of Judas
that must betray you.
                              (My
parentheses are exhausted.) Almighty
pseudonym, grant me at last,
as the token of my belief,
such ability to remain
silent, as is the nearest to a reflection
of your silence to which
the human looking-glass may attain.


*Sanctus*

The bunsen flame burns and is not consumed,
and the scientist has not removed his shoes
because the ground is not holy.

And because the financiers' sun
is not Blake's sun, there is a
word missing from the dawn chorus.

Yet without subsidies poetry
sings on, celebrating the heart
and the 'holiness of its affections'.

And one listens and must not listen
in vain for the not too clinical
sanctus that is as the halo of its transplanting.

## Benedictus

Blessed be the starved womb
and the replete womb.

Blessed the slug in the dew
and the butterfly among the ash-cans.

Blessed the mind that brings forth good and bad
and the hand that exonerates it.

Blessed be the adder among its jewels
and the child ignorant of how love must pay.

Blessed the hare who, in a round
world, keeps the tortoise in sight.

Blessed the cross warning: No through road,
and that other Cross with its arms out pointing both ways.

Blessed the woman who is amused
at Adam feeling for his lost rib.

Blessed the clock with its hands over its face
pretending it is midday, when it is midnight.

Blessed be the far side of the Cross and the back
of the mirror, that they are concealed from us.

## Agnus Dei

No longer the Lamb
but the idea of it.
Can an idea bleed?
On what altar
does one sacrifice an idea?

It gave its life
for the world? No,
it is we give our life
for the idea that nourishes
itself on the dust in our veins.

God is love. Where
there is no love, no God?
There is only the gap between
word and deed we try
narrowing with an idea.

## Stations

It is an old story:
the ship that was here last night
gone this morning; love
here one moment not here
any more. Time with a reputation
for transience permanent
as the ring in the rock
on beaches that would persuade
us we are the first comers.

We have been here before
and failed, bringing creation
about our ears. Why
can we not be taught
there is no hill beyond this one
we roll our minds to the top
of, not to take off into
empty space, nor to be cast back down
where we began, but to hold the position
assigned to us, long as time
lasts, somewhere half-way
up between earth and heaven.

## Adam Tempted

Did Adam dream of the north pole,
the south pole, with Eve's equator
between them, inflammatory to cross?
And whose was the voice that whispered
to him: 'Stay here'? Where was
here? When now? Too fidgety
the mind's compass, too unreliable
the waterclock of the blood.

And yet he set out, himself
his direction, exchanging wisdom
by the way for the heart's moments.

A slow traveller with all time
to arrive but for the machine's smiling
undertaking to get him there sooner.

## First Person

Whisperings we dare not turn
into a voice; insinuations
of godhead; able to address
him as though he were not other.

It is the answer to imponderable
questions. Since we were here
always, we need not die but only
remember. It is the nominative

that is important. This was the spirit
brooding on the face of the waters,
knowing there would be no reflection
there other than of itself.

Sin happens, pain happens, when we forget
who we are, descending deep
into the flesh without the Golden Bough
as our guide. They are the penalties

of division, a surrender to the belief
that we are not whole. The scientist
brings his lenses to bear and unity
is fragmented. It is the hand saying

it is not of the body, leaving it
to the poet, playing upon his timeless
instrument, to call all things back
into irradiated orbit about the one word.

## One Day

In that day language
shall expose its sores,
begging for the alms
we can not give. 'Leave it'
we shall say, 'on the pavement
of the quotidian.' There is
a cause there is nobody
to plead, yet whose sealed lips
are its credentials. What
does the traveller to your door
ask, but that you sit down
and share with him that
for which there are no words?
I look forward to the peace
conferences of the future
when lies, hidden behind speeches,
shall have their smiles blown away
by the dove's wings, fanning in silence.

# Requests

To the angel without wings:
'Greetings; don't let me keep you.'

To the winged one, making as if
to be up and gone: 'Stay awhile.'

To the dark angel, pedlar
of reflections: 'I am not at home.'

To the one sworn eternally
to silence: 'Eavesdrop my heart.'

To truth's angel: 'In his ear about me
nothing but the white lie.'

# Nativity

Christmas Eve! Five
hundred poets waited, pen
poised above paper,
for the poem to arrive,
bells ringing. It was because
the chimney was too small,
because they had ceased
to believe, the poem passed them
by on its way out
into oblivion, leaving
the doorstep bare
of all but the sky-rhyming
child to whom later
on they would teach prose.

## Questions to the Prophet

How will the lion remain a lion
if it eat straw like the ox?

Where will the little child lead them
who has not been there before?

With our right hand off, with what
shall we beg forgiveness in the kingdom?

How shall the hare know it has not won,
dying before the tortoise arrive?

Did Christ crying: 'Neither do I condemn thee',
condemn the prostitute to be good for nothing?

If he who increases riches increases sorrow
why are his tears more like pearls than the swine's tusks?

## Retired

Not to worry myself any more
if I am out of step, fallen behind.
Let the space probes continue;
I have a different distance to travel.

Here I can watch the night sky,
listen to how one grass blade
grates on another as member
of a disdained orchestra.

There are no meetings to attend
now other than those nocturnal
gatherings, whose luminaries
fell silent millenia ago.

No longer guilty of wasting
my time, I take my place
by a lily-flower, believing
with Blake that when God comes

he comes sometimes by way
of the nostril. My failure, perhaps,
was to have had no sense of smell
for the holiness suspiring from forked humans.

I count over the hours put by
for repentance, pulling thought's buildings
down to make way for the new,
fooling myself with the assurance

that when he occurs it is as the weather
of prayer's forecast, never with all
the unexpectedness of his body's
lightning, naked upon a cross.

## Not Blonde

The Iron Lady became
rusty. Generals haunted
unstaffed corridors, clanking
their medals. On the imagination's

barbed wire a dove sat,
its eye red as the poppies
that were being hawked in aid
of casualties of the next war.

# The God

*Of Poets*

Made of rhyme and metre,
the ability to scan
disordered lines; an imposed
syntax; the word like a sword
turning both ways
to keep the gates of vocabulary.

*Of Musicians*

The first sound
in the silence; the frequency
of the struck chord; the electrical,
ultimate rhythm of the full
orchestra, himself the
conductor of it and the composer.

*Of Artists*

Who disguises
himself in wood and stone;
who has to be unmasked
with much patience; who escapes
in the end, leaving them standing,
tool in hand, in front of a supposition.

*Of Scientists*

The agitation at the centre
of non-being; the agreed myth
of their equations; the experiment
that proved them wrong; the
answer they have overrun
that waits for them to turn round.

*Of Theologians*

The word as an idea,
crumbled by their dry
minds in the long sentences
of their chapters, gathering dust
in their libraries; a sacrament that,
if not soon swallowed, sticks in the throat.


*Who Is*

Whose conversation
is the aside; whose mind
is its own fountain, who
overflows. Who takes the Cross
from between his teeth
to fly humanity upon it.

# The Reason

I gird myself for the agon.
And there at the beginning
is the word. What does it mean
and who initiated it?
Behind the word is the name
not to be known for fear
we should gain power over it.
It is buried under the page's
drift, and not all our tears,
not all our air-conditioning
can bring on the thaw. Our sentences
are but as footprints arrested
indefinitely on its threshold.

Perhaps our letters for it
are too many. Nearer the sound,
neither animal nor human,
drawn out through the wrenched
mouth of the oracle at Delphi.
Nearer the cipher the Christ
wrote on the ground, with no one
without sin to peer at it
over his shoulder.
                        Male
as I am, my place, perhaps,
is to sit down in a mysterious
presence, leaving the vocabularies
to toil, the machine to eviscerate
its resources; learning we are here
not necessarily to read on,
but to explore with blind
fingers the word in the cold,
until the snow turn to feathers
and somewhere far down we come
upon warmth and a heart beating.

## Journeys

The deception of platforms
where the arrivals and the departures
coincide. And the smiles
on the faces of those welcoming

and bidding farewell are
to conceal the knowledge
that destinations are the familiarities
from which the traveller must set out.

## Nuptials

Like a bird he sang,
when they were married,
on a branch of his own
prospects. Farewell, farewell
to the girls who had
refused him, celebrating
his mistake. Did she listen
to him, plaiting the basket
from which he would take
bread? Once the whole loaf:
flesh white, breasts risen
to his first kneading;
a slice after, the appetite
whetted for the more
not to be; the fast
upon fast to be broken
only in love's absence
by the crumb of a kiss.

MONBRIDGE SCHOOL
LIBRARY

# Plas-yn-Rhiw

By day it is its own
audience. By night
its lights turn
to sores in the mist.

I have eavesdropped it
too long. It has nothing
to teach but that time
is the spirit's privation.

Memories are voracious.
What is left of my
life after, each day,
they have had their meal?

Morning or evening
up and down between
box on the worn
carpet of my patience.

Faces on long stems
remind. Bird voices
recall, charitable but
shrill...the velvet band

round the throat purring
with complacence. The place
itself is a memorial
to the peremptoriness

of emotions I have nothing
to bring to but pressed
flowers. The century
closes. The writing

of the lichen is too slow
for mind to attend
to. The sky modernises
its cipher and the orchard

where time dozed is
a laboratory for experimenting
with life's seed, where chromosomes
are divided, genes crossed

with genes, and God
shuts his eyes for mutations
to come up with a new
colouring for thought's apple.

# Preference

The mythology of a species:
Jesus Christ? Muhamad? But only
the wind is real. We have tried
personalising it as divine breath,

but the answer of the universe
is 'OM! OM!' I have visited
the nurseries, seen childhood
revelling among tame

toys. Outside were the stars
that made shapes before
language began. The scientists teach
the possibility of thinking

without words. Their god
is the old nameless god
of calculus and inertia.
I understand rounded space,

time that is irreversible.
I have wakened in the night,
my hair rising at the passing
of presences that were not human;

switched on the light on articles
and upholstery, and switched it as soon
off in preference for the dark places
to the certainty of our domestication.

# Portrait

Speaking always with that
restraint that was itself
an excess. Smiling at us
so as to conceal tears.

Waiting so far ahead
in modesty for us to catch
up as to appear forward.
Apologising for the time

invested in her, considering
it without interest. Hostess
of life, as unable to help
herself as if she were its guest.

# Aside

Cold beach, solitary
sea with its monotone
on the shingle; the ring
in the rock prohibiting
the conviction that no one
has been here before.

Man, is there anywhere
you can say this, peering
into the future under
the mushroom cloud? Mixed
with our oldest bones are
disturbing relics, too contemporary
to be there. In pre-history
someone came to this threshold
on which you hesitate
and crossed it, incinerating
the planet, leaving it
to life to lick its wounds
thousands of years. Thought
is as fast as light,
to exceed that brings annihilation
upon us.
        Yet wisdom
is at our elbow, whispering,
as at his once: Progress
is not with the machine;
it is a turning aside,
a bending over a still pool,
where the bubbles arise
from unseen depths, as from truth
breathing, showing us by their roundness
the roundness of our world.

# R.I.P.

*1588–1988*


And the Englishman asks:
How do you say it? twitching
his nostril at the odiousness
of comparisons between a Welsh
village and capital of the world
as instruments of salvation.

It is off the main road
even to market; nothing to induce
the traveller to a digression
but rumours of the tumbling
of water out of the sky
copiously as grace pouring

to irrigate the hearts
of a people that had grown arid
as much from the law's bones
they were fed on, as from
the anarchy on their borders
desiccating charity in its east wind.

    If he was incumbent,
    there was a responsibility also
    incumbent upon him.

    The river was the mill-
    water turning his pen
    to the grinding of Hebrew

    to Welsh corn, now flooding
    him with vocabulary,
    now smooth enough for the dancing

    of his mind's fly time
    and again on its surface,
    angling for the right word.

We are inheritors
of his catch. He invested
his haul, so readers to come

should live off the interest.
Imagine his delight
in striking those Welsh nouns,

as they rose from the shadows,
that are alive as ever
stippling the book's page.

It was not always success.
The hills are high; asking their question
too sharply, they met the iciness
of a reply. Language can be
like iron. Are we sure we can bend
the Absolute to our meaning?

When the moon rises, beautiful
and indifferent, its reflection
in windows is as of his face
staring from an asylum of thought.
To be so near, and to be as far off
as Andromeda; this is torment.

History has no camera,
so his photograph waits
on the imagination. Let
me take it for you,

unemphatic about
features, but crinkling the lips
with Welsh humour at the thought
the book was to be used

for the promotion of English.
A face with irony's
inaudible laughter tickling
it: this is for your album.

Is an obsession with language
an acknowledgement we are too late
to save it? It has been infiltrated
already by daub and symbol.
We are graduates of the cartoon,
victims of the subliminal
coaxing of smiles and colours.
Now four hundred years in arrears
with our rent, we prefer a pilgrimage
to a birth-place, contributing generously
to a memorial, preparing to go
backward in time up long lanes,
through Welsh weather, to condescend
for an hour to listen to an outmoded
language's congratulation of itself.

       In the beginning
       was the word. What
       word? At the end
       is the dust. We know
       what dust; the dust
       that the bone comes to,
       that is the fall-out
       from our hubris, the
       dust on the Book
       that, out of breath
       with our hurry
       we dare not blow off
       in a cloud, lest out
       of that cloud should
       be resurrected the one
       spoken figure we have grown
       too clever to believe in.

# Hark

You were wrong, Narcissus.
The replica of the self
is to be avoided. Echo
was right, warning you against

the malevolence of mirrors.
Yet the scientist still bends
over his cloning, call as she may,
irrefutable beside the gene-pool.

# Come Down

A peasantry on its knees,
not praying, labouring
for the bread that perishes.

And this one came preaching
the gospel of folly
that man shall not live

by bread only. So they left
the fields to assist
at the delivery of the machine

from time's side. Of whom
does the scarecrow remind
arms wide as though pierced

by the rain's nails, while
the motorist goes by insolently
wagging his speedometer's finger?

# The Refusal

First it was gilled man,
then man quadruped,
man erect, peering
without recognising it
at his future. Losing trust
in the present he invented
the chronometer to go faster.
Mobile man, wheeled man,
man trying to keep up
with himself. Vocabulary toiled
behind science, behind music,
the brush.
        I have seen
the winged man, and he was no
angel. Was there a turning
he missed, where resources
could have been stored
by watching without envy
the directionless accelerations?

There is no answer other
than that it is too late to be saved
by the multitude of our questions.
Begrudging us our tenancy
of a remote peace, they make
our periphery their centre
through speed and noise. Wringing
our hands, we wring our belief
dry, refusing from pride
or shame after the failure
of our specifics the one cultivable
remedy the intellect disdains.

# Winter

Evening. A fire
in the grate and a fire
outside, where a robin
is burning. How they both
sing, offering a friendship
unacceptable to the hand
that is as vulnerable to the one
as it is treacherous to the other.

Ah, time, enemy of their music,
reducing fuel to feathers, feathers
to ash, it was, but a moment ago,
spring in this tinder: flames
in flower that are now embers
on song's hearth.
                          The leaves fall
from a dark tree, brimming
with shadow, fall on one who,
as Borges suggested,
is no more perhaps than the dream God
in his loneliness is dreaming.

# Question

Credibly in an age of doubt
advancing up to the rim
and finding oneself on the far
side, finding that the abyss
is nothing because it is nothing
but an idea. We have been victims
of vocabulary for too long.
The one hope for the future
is that our inventions will
have outstripped it. In the absence
of terms what after-life is there
for the furies? The instrument illustrates
what it is for. It is the dictionary
deceives us. Woman, whose statistics
are for the diversion of the computer,
why the sudden shambles of your face,
but that I have told you I love you?

# Tidal

The waves run up the shore
and fall back. I run
up the approaches of God
and fall back. The breakers return
reaching a little further,
gnawing away at the main land.
They have done this thousands
of years, exposing little by little
the rock under the soil's face.
I must imitate them only
in my return to the assault,
not in their violence. Dashing
my prayers at him will achieve
little other than the exposure
of the rock under his surface.
My returns must be made
on my knees. Let despair be known
as my ebb-tide; but let prayer
have its springs, too, brimming,
disarming him; discovering somewhere
among his fissures deposits of mercy
where trust may take root and grow.

## Match My Moments

That time
the soldier broke in
to my room and I,
the sword at my throat,
looked up from my sums
and theorems and smiling
said: Spare my designs.

That time
in the rusting bracken
the road ran with sheep,
a woollen river but vocal,
saying in its raw baritone
to the man on its banks:
We give our life for the shepherd.

That time
the queue winding towards
the gas chambers, and the nun,
who had already died
to this world, to the girl
in tears: Don't cry. Look,
I will take your place.

That time
after the night's frost the tree
weeping, the miser in me
complaining: Why all this washing
the earth's feet in gold? And I,
my finger at my lips: Because
it is what we are made of.

# Healing

Sick wards. The sailed beds
becalmed. The nurses tack
hither and fro. The chloroform
breeze rises and falls.
Hospitals are their own
weather. The temperatures
have no relation
to the world outside. The surgeons,
those cunning masters
of navigation, follow
their scalpels' compass through
hurricanes of pain to a calm
harbour. Somewhere far down
in the patient's darkness,
where faith died, like a graft
or a transplant prayer
gets to work, repairing
the soul's tissue, leading
the astonished self between
twin pillars, where life's angels
stand wielding their bright swords of flame.

# Tell Us

We have had names for you:
The Thunderer, the Almighty
Hunter, Lord of the snowflake
and the sabre-toothed tiger.
One name we have held back
unable to reconcile it
with the mosquito, the tidal-wave,
the black hole into which
time will fall. You have answered
us with the image of yourself
on a hewn tree, suffering
injustice, pardoning it;
pointing as though in either
direction; horrifying us
with the possibility of dislocation.
Ah, love, with your arms out
wide, tell us how much more
they must still be stretched
to embrace a universe drawing
away from us at the speed of light.

# Markers

Wittgenstein's signposts pointing
at the boundaries of language
into the obligatory void.

Laplace, hypothetically
unembarrassed, the self-made thinker's
bravado in front of a condescension.

Hume, bumping his mind
so often against a cause,
as to become insensible of its presence.

Descartes thinking he could think
Descartes, but what he thought were
the co-respondents in a divorce.

Buridan's ass? No, a catalepsy
of time at the thought of the narrowing
of the interval between two mouthfuls.

To where it began: Plato jilting
the one truth at his side for the shadowless
idea of it ogling him from Parnassus.

# Eschatology

It was our last inter-glacial:
the flies, people,
the one as numerous
as the other. We talked
peace, and brought our arms up to date.
The young ones professed
love, embarrassing themselves
with their language. As though
coming round on a new
gyre, we approached God
from the far side, an extinct concept.
No one returned from our space
probes, yet still there were
volunteers, believing that as
gravity slackened its hold
on the body, so would time
on the mind. Our scientists,
immaculately dressed not
conceived, preached to us
from their space-stations, calling us
to consider the clockwork birds
and fabricated lilies, how they
also, as they were conditioned to
do, were neither toiling nor spinning.

## Circles

Old men looked back, the young
forward. What did it matter
in a round world? Love
and truth kept their place

on the horizon. The war
that was won was for fighting
again. As though their main
hope was the electron

men crowded a glass
waiting for it to break
out into a new orbit,
ignoring the poet

who, from the rope-trick
of the language, called down
like an angel stranded
somewhere between earth and heaven.

# Monday's Child...

MONDAY:      Unclouded. The smiles
beating down, the brow clear.
Eyes, nose, mouth add up
to a total beyond sex.

TUESDAY:      Brim-full of it
as a vessel inexhaustibly
to be drunk from. A scent
given off, as though
the purveyor of it were a flower.

WEDNESDAY:  Let down at birth
into a dark well and
overflowing with it. To have
all this to spare, and the heart empty.

THURSDAY:    The horizon recedes from
him. It is truth's mirage.
He was born travelling.
Is it because he is addressed
quietly, the voices seem to be far off?

FRIDAY:        Replenished equally
with its distribution.
Turning its last crumb into
a meal for thousands.
Accepting the shark's tooth,
the ravening virus,
as necessary extravagances
in the economy of God.

SATURDAY:    To the bone, whether
in thought or action;
the mind's grindstone
turning all night, the flesh
put day after day
to the same hurdle;
the wages accumulating
to keep body and soul asunder.

SUNDAY:     Affluence without
            inflation; as good
            as gold. Interpreter
            to the serpent, medicating
            its venom. Riding to life,
            head high, with a dove on its fist.

# The Un-born

I have seen the child in the womb,
neither asking to be born
or not to be born, biding its time
without the knowledge of time,
model for the sculptor who would depict
the tranquillity that inheres
before thought, or the purity of thought
without language. Its smile forgave
the anachronism of the nomenclature
that would keep it foetal. Its hands
opened delicately as flowers
in innocency's garden, ignorant
of the hands growing to gather them
for innocency's grave.
Was its part written? I have seen
it waiting breathlessly in the wings
to come forth on to a stage
of soil or concrete, where wings
are a memory only or an aspiration.

## Sure

Where the lamb died
a bird sings.
Where a soul perishes
what music? The cross

is an old-fashioned
weapon, but its bow
is drawn unerringly
against the heart.

# Could Be

The voice that was
as the remains of a smile
on the sky's face said:
'Listen.' And I replied:
'I know. You are the ventriloquist
who once sat Christ
on your knee and made us imagine
you were where you were not.

Will you continue to torment us?
If you are ubiquitous, why
not be here, when we say: Now?
The electron's confinement gives
birth to excess of speed.
You, who are without limits,
are exempt from time and could move,
if you wished, so gradually
about your being as to appear
to us, when we are furthest off, always
to be in the same place.'

# Time

The pessimist says: Time
goes; the optimist: It is coming.

What is this thing, time?
Let Augustine be our spokesman.

Its competitor knows its neurosis;
the lover the dragging of its chained feet.

Now, we say, looking at the moon
that is the sun in Australia.

We keep saving it for the future
and arriving there are insolvent.

Young, our hobby was assassinating it.
Old we pray for its recuperation.

# One Life

Growing up
is to leave the fireside
with its tales,
the burying of the head
between God's knees.
It is to perceive
that knowledge of him comes
from the genes' breaking
of an involved code,
from the mind's parallel
at-homeness with missile and scalpel.

Literature is on the way
out. The still, small voice
is that of Orpheus looking
over his shoulder at a dream
fading. At the mouth
of the cave is the machine's
whirlwind, hurrying the new
arts in, advancing the threshold
of our permitted exposure to
its becquerels and decibels.

## Something More

You remain contented
        with your anonymity.
We ask for survival
        for John Jones.
We acknowledge the tree
        that at moments
you are ablaze in,
           taking our shoes
      off, involuntarily remembering
there is dung at its roots.

They say there is a pool
        at the bottom of which
you lie, and that we ourselves
           are the troublers
of its surface. But why,
      when we look down,
          is it as though
we looked up at our own faces
at home there among the cloud branches?

# I

Kierkegaard hinted, Heidegger
agreed: the nominative
is God, a clearing
in thought's forest where truth

breathes, coming at us
like light itself, now
in waves from a great distance,
now in the intimacy of our corpuscles.

# Bleak Liturgies

Shall we revise the language?
And in revising the language
will we alter the doctrine?

Do we seek to plug the hole
in faith with faith's substitute
grammar? And are we to be saved

by translation? As one by one
the witnesses died off
they commended their metaphors

to our notice. For two thousand
years the simplistic recipients
of the message pointed towards

the reductionist solution. We devise
an idiom more compatible with
the furniture departments of our churches.

Instead of the altar
the pulpit. Instead
of the bread the fraction
of the language. And God
a shadow of himself
on a blank wall. Their prayers
are a passing of hands
over their brows as though
in an effort to wipe sin
off. Their buildings
are in praise of concrete
and macadam. Frowning
upon divorce, they divorce
art and religion.
Ah, if one flower
had been allowed to grow
between the wall

and the railings as sacrament
of renewal. Instead
two cypresses ail
there, emaciated as the bodies
of the thieves upon Calvary
but with no Saviour between them.


'Alms. Alms. By Christ's
blood I conjure you

a penny.' On saints'
days the cross and

shackles were the jewellery
of the rich. As God

aged, kings laundered their feet
in the tears of the poor.


'Come,' life said
leading me on a journey
as long as that
of the wise men to the cradle,

where, in place of the child
it had brought forth,
there lay grinning the lubricated
changeling of the machine.


Where to turn? To whom
to appeal? The prayer probes
have been launched and silence
closes behind them. The Amens
are rents in the worn fabric
of meaning. Are we
our own answer? Is
to grow up to destroy
childhood's painting of one

who was nothing but vocabulary's
shadow? Where do the stone
faces come from but from
trying to meet the sky's
empty stare? The sermon
was too long. These thoughts
flew in and out of windows
he had not bothered to look through.

The missionaries arrive now
by fast jet. Salvation accelerates
with the times. It is a race between
Jesus and Lenin to become
high-priest at the administering
of the chrism. Science analyses
the real presence. Crosses
are mass-produced to be worn
on punk chests. Theology
connives at politics' removal
of one word from Article
three seven. The hierarchy in keeping
its head has no heart for the baptism
of love and lust's Siamese twins.

The gaps in belief are filled
with ceremonies and processions.
The organ's whirlwind follows
upon the still, small voice

of conviction, and he is not
in it. Our marriage
was contracted in front
of a green altar in technology's

childhood, and light entered
through the plain glass of
the wood's window as quietly
as a shepherd moving among his flock.

Faith can remove mountains.
        So can cordite. But faith
heals. So does valium's
        loosening of the taut nerves.

Three days the Electoral
        College waited for the Holy
Spirit to come to terms
        with the media's prediction.

Too cynical. Quantum mechanics
        restores freedom to the cowed
mind that, winking at matter,
        causes it to wink back.


        What Lent is the machine
        subjected to? It neither fasts
        nor prays. And the one cross
        of its Good Fridays is the change

        over of its gears. Its Easter
        is every day when, from the darkness
        of man's mind, it comes forth
        in a new form, but untouchable as ever.


Must the Church also
        suffer a mutation?
The communicants' jeans,
        the whiskered faces with

their imitation of Christ?
        Re-editing the scriptures
we come on a verse suggesting
        that we be gay, so gay we are.

His defences are in depth, then?
Behind the molecules are the electrons,
behind those the leptons and quarks.

And when the computers that are our spies
have opened to us from inside
he is not there; the walls fall apart

and there are only the distances
stretching away. We have captured position
after position, and his white flag

is a star receding from us
at light's speed. Is there another way
of engaging? There are those who,

thinking of him in the small hours
as eavesdropping their hearts
and challenging him to come forth,

have found, as the day dawned,
his body hanging upon the crossed tree
of man, as though he were man, too.

IONBRIDGE SCHOOL
LIBRARY

# The Price

So many wise men
all of them helpless.
       And the strong
foolish and persuasive,
buying the consciences off,
       putting their faith
in the invulnerability of old spectres;
graduates of the colleges
of untruth, denying the connection
between power and cash.
And art sits on the pavement,
its cap full of the dead leaves
of the autumn of a culture. Eheu
fugaces! The scientist scribbles
       over the archaism
with his surds and equations;
while eloquence gutters
in the draught out of the empty
pews, whispering to the defenders
of the indefensible: The price
of eternal vigilance is our freedom.

# Moth

Big enough to be
noticed, small enough

to escape, it embodies
in winged dust life's

earliest principle
which is to exist

without asking. I
clap and it rises

on unseen currents,
belittling my thunder.

After the human
storm it will pursue

its business, fretting,
fretting away without

a tear at the material
on which it depends.

## Target

I look up at the sky at night
and see the archer, Sagittarius,
with his bow drawn, and realise
man is the arrow speeding,

not as some think infinitely
on, but because space is curved,
backwards towards the bowman's heart
to deal him his unstanched wound.

# The Seasons

## *Spring*

The spirit sang on the bone
to the blood that was in
me, and many as flowers
thought seeded and grew
words in the mind's garden –
the promise of language!
I was the poet coming
to it for its nectar. I fed
full on the ambivalences of honey.
I built high in my branches,
augury of a serene summer.
Love fledged and was no migrant
but resident and identified
by the unreasonableness of its music.

## *Summer*

Everywhere pattern;
design without a designer?
I gather a bird's feather
which looks at me in
silence and tells all.

In every member of
its species the same eye
will be found in the same
barbules, saying nothing,
informing us who it is.

It is the summer of
the plumage. Like fruit
ripening, ready to fall,
the feather brightens towards
harvest and lets go.

There is an August
within us, aeons
of preparation for a few
kingfisher days. We fly
the diameter of a circle.

She was the colour
of corn. Fine wheat
was her texture. Somewhere
within her, palpitating,
was the heart's poppy.


*Autumn*

Happy the leaves
burnishing their own
downfall. Life dances
upon life's grave.
It is we who inject
sadness into the migrant's
cry. We are so long
in dying – time granted
to discover a purpose
in our decay? Could
we be cut open,
would there be more than
the saw's wound, all
humanity's rings widening
only towards ageing?
To creep in for shelter
under the bone's tree
is to be charred by time's
lightning stroke. The leaves
fall variously as do thoughts
to reveal the bareness
of the mind's landscape
through which we must press on
towards the openness of its horizons.

*Winter*

The machine is
our winter, smooth
as ice glassing
over the soul's surface.

We have looked
it in the eye
and seen how our image
gradually is demoted.

Without the tribute
we must bring it
from our dwindling resources
it grows colder and colder.

It is our January
and our December,
a two-faced God
on an unreal threshold

directing its eyes back
at the hand's blindness,
but forward also towards
the defeat of time.

# Annunciation

She came like a saint
to her bride-bed, hands
clasped, mind clenched
on a promise. 'Some

fell by the wayside,'
she whispered. 'Come, birds,
winnow the seed lest,
standing beside a chaste

cradle with a star
over it, I see flesh
as snow fallen and think
myself mother of God.'

# The Word

Enough that we are on our way;
never ask of us where.

Some of us run, some loiter;
some of us turn aside

to erect the Calvary
that is our signpost, arms

pointing in opposite directions
to bring us in the end

to the same place, so impossible
is it to escape love. Imperishable

scarecrow, recipient of our casts-off,
shame us until what is a swear-

word only becomes at last
the word that was in the beginning.

# Pen Llŷn

Dafydd looked out;
I look out: five centuries
without change? The same sea breaks
on the same shore and is not
broken. The stone in Llŷn
is still there, honey-
coloured for a girl's hair
to resemble. It is time's
smile on the cliff
face at the childishness
of my surprise. Here was the marriage
of land and sea, from whose bickering
the spray rises. 'Are you there?'
I call into the dumb
past, that is close to me
as my shadow. 'Are you here?'
I whisper to the encountered
self like one coming
on the truth asleep
and fearing to disturb it.

# Jaromir Hladik

And with the passing of the years
the flesh following
the genetic coding brought forth
Borges who, blind, saw
in the darkness at the centre
the great soul that did not know
who it was. What genealogy
has the self other
than the wisdom gathered
from standing so often
before time's firing
squad, computing its
eternity in the triggered interval
before the command to shoot?

## A Marriage

We met
        under a shower
of bird-notes.
        Fifty years passed,
love's moment
        in a world in
servitude to time.
        She was young;
I kissed with my eyes
        closed and opened
them on her wrinkles.
        'Come' said death,
choosing her as his
        partner for
the last dance. And she,
        who in life
had done everything
        with a bird's grace,
opened her bill now
        for the shedding
of one sigh no
        heavier than a feather.

# What Then?

You chose the natural timber
to die on that the natural
man should be saved. What boughs,
then, will need to be crossed
and what body crucified
upon them for salvation
to be won for the astronauts
venturing in their air-conditioned
capsules? Will artificial living
give birth to the artificial
sin? What prayers will they say
upside down in their space-chambers?
Are you prepared to reveal
the nuclear brain and the asbestos
countenance to deserve their worship?
They are planning their new conurbations
a little nearer the stars,
incinerated by day and by night
glacial; but will there be room there
for a garden for the Judas
of the future to make his way through
to give you his irradiated kiss?

# Newts

In a pool
on the mountain
newts live, semi-
palmated, grey-faced
as stone; reptilian
gargoyles on cornices
of water. Their world
stretches from horizon
to horizon, which is
two feet by two.
            Here
everything happens:
pain, bliss, hunger –
but what are a newt's
thoughts? Their brows corrugated
from long pondering
a scaled truth they rest
panting like life itself
on the wondering journey
that is without end.

# The Letter

I look up from my book,
from the unreality of language,
and stare at the sea's surface
that says nothing and means it.

This morning there came this letter
from the heart's stranger, promising
to pray for me. What does that
mean? I, who am a man of prayer,

ask and am silent. Would he
make me insolvent? Strip me
of initiatives in order to repay
trust? Must I refrain from walking

this same sea, lest sinking
I should deride him? Operate
my vehicle at no speed
to attribute to him the safety

in which I arrive? I think his god
is not my god, or he would not
ask for such things. I admit
he has driven me to my knees

but with my eyes open so that,
by long looking over concealed
fathoms, I gaze myself into accepting
that to pray true is to say nothing.

# The Lost

Mourners after the shadows
they are deprived of
by an absence of light.

Speak to them, they will not
hear. Write them letters,
they will not receive them.

Their address is the darkness
behind the mirrors
their captors confront us with.

They are nothing, nobody,
sunk to their knees not
in prayer; mouths opening

not for converse, for offal
the guards administer them
with to prolong their anguish.

Go your way. Comfort
yourself with the reminder
you can do nothing.

They are beyond the reach
even of an Amen. The Grand
Inquisitor's countenance

is averted. Jesus'
too? The bread of the one
and the freedom of the other

offer no more light
to the nameless than does
the mildew forming upon both.

# Afon Rhiw

Its methods were not sweeping
away, but by a continual plucking
to make one lose one's hold
on its stones. Its character
was that of thought: smooth
brow with behind it the trout
rising and disappearing swiftly
as an idea. I angled
for them, dandling a fly
between one depth and another,
hoping for the mandala
to come to the surface to concentrate
the mind. What is existence
but standing patiently for a while
amid flux? Mostly the fish
nibbled and were gone, singing
mistily out of my reach.
The fly soared, drying its wings
in the March wind before
redoubling its temptations,
offering like life itself
a hook hidden among feathers.

Let me tell you that without
catching a thing I was not far
from the truth that time, since meaning
is not in having but trying.
Questioned, the trout had confessed
I was indistinguishable
from a tree, roots in darkness
my head in the clouds, and that
like thoughts, too, their best place
was among the shadows rather
than being drawn into the light's
dryness to perish of too much air.

## Migrants

He is that great void
we must enter, calling
to one another on our way
in the direction from which
he blows. What matter
if we should never arrive
to breed or to winter
in the climate of our conception?

Enough we have been given wings
and a needle in the mind
to respond to his bleak north.
There are times even at the Pole
when he, too, pauses in his withdrawal,
so that it is light there all night long.

# Sonata in X

ADAM:   'What's that you've got on?'
EVE:     'Nothing. Why?'
ADAM:   'I could have sworn.'
EVE:     'Don't do that. Here, taste.'
ADAM:   'H'm! Who gave it you?'
EVE:     'He flowed. Look – like this.'
ADAM:   'Whereas I am erect, rigid.
          But listen...What's that?'

Some said: 'The voice of a god.'
And others, it thundered.
Ever since then two
minds, and reason between them,
pendulum of a stopped
clock. If what is true
is not fair, how can
what is fair, then, be true?

I woke up
looked through the eye
of the needle of the rich
man found the view
to my taste climbed into
the tree of the knowledge
of good and evil to add
to my stature stood
in my own light admiring
my shadow   and one
spoke to me there of
my one talent urging
investment the usury
of the spirit but I looked
out over the wall
of the garden where grapes grew
upon thorns and the machine
gathered them so that the children's
dentures were not set on edge.

Waking and wondering
when was I and where
had I been? Standing back

from myself, beginning to recall
uterine experience,
an antiphonal music

in infinite counterpoint
between mirror and mirror.
Time was technology's

folk-tale. My introspection
could have been called a navel
engagement; the truth my ability

to hold all things in play;
bringing beauty to birth
out of my unbreached side.

My apostrophes were to myself
only. I found, when I leaned
closer, the second person

did not exist. Vertical in my
dimensionless presence I kept calling
to the undying echoes: 'Prove that I lie.'


There was something I was near
and never attained: a pattern,
an explanation. Why did I address it
in person? The evolutionists told
me I was wrong. My premises,
the philosophers assured me,
were incorrect. Perpendicular
I agreed, but on my knees
looking up, cap in hand,
at the night sky I laid astronomy
on one side. These were the spiritual
conurbations illuminated always
by love's breath; a colonising
of the far side of the mind
without loss of the openness of its spaces.

The foolish ones bred
all the time,
the wise in the intervals
between wars; their children came

to the same end. The poet took notice
of this, but lacked rhyme
to express it, and his prosody
was out of date. History

has nothing to teach, nor humanity
to learn. Our lessons are done
out of school in the church-
yard under the owl's cry.


Maggots, I thought, how like bread
they are, crumbled;
yet it is they who eat
us and not we them.

In flight's cause we perish.

There is a sacrament of death, too.


Arguing since Plato's
day: Does the tune exist
when the instruments are
silent? If we could solve

that, there would be nothing to do
but sing in the crab's ear,
beside the gene-pool, at the re-installed
tables of the money changers.


He never asked himself what was sin,
but, challenged, would have replied:
'The neutrality of the affections.'

He never enquired what was power,
but drank from it insatiably
as a looking-glass drinks at the conscience.

She never sought an argument
for behaviour but arrowed her glances
impenitently as her mood blew.

She was mixed ground for the sowing
of such seed as, grown tall, would
declare for righteousness and betray it.


What poet, scientist,
musician ever arrived

who was behind the times?
Last night I crept up on him

in the dark. This morning
there is only the bone's sand

with the footprints the oncoming
tide is erasing one by one.


'I love you.'
'How much?'
'$1^{32}$ x $\sqrt{-1}$.'
'Wait a minute, let me
compute my thanks.
     There.
Meet me tonight
at SH 126 243
so we may
consummate our statistics.'


Galileo's lens, so long idle,
has become the peep-hole
of time, crowded with faces,
voyeurs of the spirit's
adultery with the machine.

See the black lightning
of its tongue, followed
by the thunder in my veins.
Ah, bright god, so near

to the ground, do you still tempt
me from behind a flower
to put out my glad hand
for the toothsomeness that is anguish?

Man, two
million years at
his back – parvenu.

Kestrel,
older, arrested
permanently in its ascent.

Rock of
no age, its hundred-weights
fortuitously poised.

Now! Man,
car, rock in the high
pass keeping an appointment.

Witness?
The kestrel in the sky
burning, but not to tell.

ALSO FROM BLOODAXE BOOKS

# Counterpoint
BY
## R.S. THOMAS

R.S. Thomas's recent collection *Counterpoint* (1990) shows him – now in his seventies – again breaking new ground. The themes are familiar, but are given a pointed, contemporary significance: the challenge of scientific knowledge, the threat to the environment, language and the machine age, a mirrored self-consciousness over the act of writing and the stuff of language, and more traditionally, love and waiting and stillness.

*Counterpoint* is a visionary work, questioning the givenness of God against a suffering world. The bleak Welsh landscape of his earlier work has become a battleground for the questing spirit and the questioning mind. As his poems have grown more austere, more pared down to essentials, Thomas has built them into different shaped collections. Yet the setting of *Counterpoint* is quite unexpected: it is the biblical structure of reality...B.C...Incarnation...Crucifixion ...A.D.

The melody of the familiar biblical tune is pitched against the melody of the unfamiliar highly personal interpretation, from the burning bush of Exodus to the 'bush of the imagination we have set on fire'. The resulting counterpoint is a scintillating challenge to the religious mind, and – because it is R.S. Thomas – kindling to the dry, contemporary soul.

'Thomas balances a ton of bleakness against the merest touch of the luminosity of a shadow...a poet-priest who has been looking the difficulties of faith harder and harder in the face...theological poems describing a metaphysical descent without bannisters' – DAVID SCOTT, *Church Times*

Paperback:   ISBN 1 85224 117 9   £6.95
Hardback:   ISBN 1 85224 116 0   £12.95

ALSO FROM BLOODAXE BOOKS

# Selected Poems
## 1946-1968
BY
# R.S. THOMAS

First published in 1973, this is R.S. Thomas's own selection from six of the finest books of poetry published since the war: *Song at the Year's Turning* (1955), *Poetry for Supper* (1958), *Tares* (1961), *The Bread of Truth* (1963), *Pietà* (1966) and *Not He That Brought Flowers* (1968). It includes many of his best-known poems, such as 'A Peasant', 'Welsh Landscape', 'Evans', 'On the Farm' and 'Reservoirs'.

'R.S. Thomas is one of the half-dozen best poets now writing in English. He often moves to tears, and certain lines of his impress themselves instantly, and perhaps ineradicably, upon the mind. His example reduces most modern verse to footling whimsy'
– KINGSLEY AMIS

'The most resolute religious poet in English this century...opposed to the materialist ethic of our present age, he remains a mystical, uncompromising seeker after unpalatable verities'
– BERNARD O'DONOGHUE, *Times Literary Supplement*

'His poetry is deeply coloured by his experience of working in remote rural communities, where some of the churches had tiny congregations and where life was harsh and the landscape bleak; he has created his own form of bleak Welsh pastoral, streaked with indignation over the history of Wales and the Welsh'
– MARGARET DRABBLE, *Oxford Companion to English Literature*

'He ranks with the greatest poets of the century and has been called the major one now writing in English. His stature is that of Yeats and Eliot' – *Western Mail*

ISBN 0 906427 96 7   £7.95

# WRITERS PUBLISHED BY
# BLOODAXE BOOKS

FLEUR ADCOCK
GÖSTA ÅGREN
ANNA AKHMATOVA
GILLIAN ALLNUTT
SIMON ARMITAGE
NEIL ASTLEY
ANNEMARIE AUSTIN
ELIZABETH BARTLETT
MARTIN BELL
CONNIE BENSLEY
STEPHEN BERG
SARA BERKELEY
ATTILIO BERTOLUCCI
YVES BONNEFOY
KARIN BOYE
KAMAU BRATHWAITE
BASIL BUNTING
CIARAN CARSON
JOHN CASSIDY
AIMÉ CÉSAIRE
SID CHAPLIN
RENÉ CHAR
GEORGE CHARLTON
EILÉAN NÍ CHUILLEANÁIN
KILLARNEY CLARY
BRENDAN CLEARY
JACK CLEMO
HARRY CLIFTON
JACK COMMON
STEWART CONN
DAVID CONSTANTINE
JANE COOPER
JENI COUZYN
HART CRANE
ADAM CZERNIAWSKI
FRED D'AGUIAR
PETER DIDSBURY
STEPHEN DOBYNS
MAURA DOOLEY
KATIE DONOVAN
JOHN DREW
IAN DUHIG
HELEN DUNMORE
JACQUES DUPIN
G.F. DUTTON
LAURIS EDMOND
ALISTAIR ELLIOT
STEVE ELLIS
ODYSSEUS ELYTIS
HANS MAGNUS
ENZENSBERGER
EURIPIDES
DAVID FERRY
EVA FIGES
SYLVA FISCHEROVÁ
TONY FLYNN

CAROLYN FORCHÉ
VICTORIA FORDE
TUA FORSSTRÖM
LINDA FRANCE
ELIZABETH GARRETT
ARTHUR GIBSON
PAMELA GILLILAN
ANDREW GREIG
CHRIS GREENHALGH
JOHN GREENING
PHILIP GROSS
MAGGIE HANNAN
JOSEF HANZLÍK
TONY HARRISON
GEOFF HATTERSLEY
ADRIAN HENRI
W.N. HERBERT
HAROLD HESLOP
DOROTHY HEWETT
SELIMA HILL
FRIEDRICH HÖLDERLIN
MIROSLAV HOLUB
FRANCES HOROVITZ
DOUGLAS HOUSTON
JOHN HUGHES
PAUL HYLAND
STEPHEN KNIGHT
PHILIPPE JACCOTTET
KATHLEEN JAMIE
VLADIMÍR JANOVIC
B.S. JOHNSON
LINTON KWESI JOHNSON
JOOLZ
JENNY JOSEPH
SYLVIA KANTARIS
JACKIE KAY
BRENDAN KENNELLY
HELEN KITSON
STEPHEN KNIGHT
JEAN HANFF KORELITZ
DENISE LEVERTOV
GWYNETH LEWIS
MARION LOMAX
EDNA LONGLEY
FEDERICO GARCÍA LORCA
PETER McDONALD
MEDBH McGUCKIAN
MAIRI MacINNES
CHRISTINE McNEILL
OSIP MANDELSTAM
GERALD MANGAN
E.A. MARKHAM
WILLIAM MARTIN
GLYN MAXWELL
HENRI MICHAUX
ADRIAN MITCHELL

JOHN MONTAGUE
EUGENIO MONTALE
DAVID MORLEY
RICHARD MURPHY
BILL NAUGHTON
HENRY NORMAL
SEAN O'BRIEN
JULIE O'CALLAGHAN
DOUGLAS OLIVER
OTTÓ ORBÁN
MICHEAL O'SIADHAIL
RUTH PADEL
GYÖRGY PETRI
TOM PICKARD
JILL PIRRIE
SIMON RAE
DEBORAH RANDALL
IRINA RATUSHINSKAYA
MARIA RAZUMOVSKY
PETER REDGROVE
ANNE ROUSE
CAROL RUMENS
LAWRENCE SAIL
EVA SALZMAN
ANN SANSOM
PETER SANSOM
SAPPHO
DAVID SCOTT
JO SHAPCOTT
SIR ROY SHAW
ELENA SHVARTS
MATT SIMPSON
LEMN SISSAY
DAVE SMITH
KEN SMITH
STEPHEN SMITH
EDITH SÖDERGRAN
PIOTR SOMMER
MARIN SORESCU
LEOPOLD STAFF
PAULINE STAINER
EIRA STENBERG
MARTIN STOKES
RABINDRANATH TAGORE
JEAN TARDIEU
D.M. THOMAS
R.S. THOMAS
TOMAS TRANSTRÖMER
MARINA TSVETAYEVA
MIRJAM TUOMINEN
FRED VOSS
NIGEL WELLS
C.K. WILLIAMS
JOHN HARTLEY WILLIAMS
JAMES WRIGHT
BENJAMIN ZEPHANIAH

*For a complete catalogue of books published by Bloodaxe, pleaee write to:*

**Bloodaxe Books Ltd, P.O. Box 1SN, Newcastle upon Tyne NE99 1SN.**

**R.S. Thomas** was born in 1913 in Cardiff and now lives in Gwynedd. He won the Heinemann Award in 1955, the Queen's Medal for Poetry in 1964, and the Cholmondeley Award in 1978, and has received the Welsh Arts Council's literature award three times.

He has published more than twenty books of poems since his first collection *The Stones of the Field* appeared in 1946, including *Selected Poems 1946-1968*, published by Bloodaxe, and its sequel *Later Poems 1972-1982* from Macmillan, publishers of his later collections *Experimenting with an Amen* (1986) and *The Echoes Return Slow* (1988). Seren Books have published two other collections, *Ingrowing Thoughts* (1985) and *Welsh Airs* (1987), as well as his *Selected Prose* (1983), Sandra Anstey's recently expanded *Critical Writings on R.S. Thomas* (1983) and J.P. Ward's study *The Poetry of R.S. Thomas* (1987).

His autobiography, *Neb*, written in Welsh, was published by Gwasg Gwynedd in 1985. His most recent poetry collections are *Counterpoint* (1990) and *Mass for Hard Times* (1992), both published by Bloodaxe. His *Collected Poems* was published by Dent in 1993.